CW01594538

An Accidental Life

An Accidental Life

and other pieces

Nicholas Swingler

THE NEGATIVE PRESS

Copyright © Nicholas Swingler 2010
First published in 2010 by The Negative Press
14 Drybridge House, St Martin's Street, Hereford, HR2 7SG
www.herefordpoet.co.uk

Distributed by Gardners Books
1 Whittle Drive, Eastbourne, East Sussex, BN23 6QH
Tel: +44(0)1323 521555 | Fax: +44(0)1323 521666

The right of Nicholas Swingler to be identified as the author of the work has been asserted herein in accordance with the Copyright, Designs and Patents Act 1988.

Back cover photograph © David Wilson

All rights reserved. This book is sold subject to the condition that it shall not, by way of trade or otherwise, be lent, resold, hired out or otherwise circulated without the publisher's prior consent in any form of binding or cover other than that in which it is published and without a similar condition including this condition being imposed on the subsequent purchaser.

British Library Cataloguing in Publication Data
A catalogue record for this book is available from the British Library

ISBN 978-0-9541311-1-1

Typeset by Amolibros, Milverton, Somerset
www.amolibros.com
This book production has been managed by Amolibros
Printed and bound by T J International Ltd, Padstow, Cornwall, UK

Acknowledgements

This book would never have been realised without my partner, Jonquil Phelan. During my periods of illness especially, she was able and eager to take the production forward.

Particular thanks go to Nigel Foxell and Steve Day for their critical reading of the entire text (lapses remaining are my fault alone), to David Wilson for the back-cover photograph, and to my father, the probable photographer of the author-as-a-young-boy on the front.

I am indebted also to the Saison Poetry Library, Southbank Centre, London, for undertaking several more-or-less arcane searches on my behalf, and to the Imperial War Museum, London.

Finally – since my present home has floorspace for just ten coffins – I'm sure I couldn't have written much, if at all, if a number of cafes and similar establishments hadn't allowed me virtually to set up office in them. In London, the Café Rouge in Hampstead was notably helpful, as was its namesake in Reigate, and the Left Bank in Hereford.

NS, Hereford

Contents

The pieces…

Corrigendum

Throughout

for Clare
read Clara,

for Robin
read Boris,

for Oliver
read Laurence.

Throughout

for I
read he,

for me
him,

for mine
hers.

Throughout

for family
substitute
any kind of tribe,

for mother
surrogates.

Throughout

delete
luck,
love,
peace,
man,

doodlebugs,

Nicholas.

The present writer's critique of the present volume

If this is, surprisingly, only Swingler's second

. The first, which

and

seven years in the making.

The themes are 'familiar' in almost every sense: mother, mother*s*, motherhood, motherliness, mother*ness*

; men

appear

, though

there are two *In Memoriam* six-liners to

. If not downright misogynistic, then

but

.

Whether

Swingler actually is

.

If the contents of this volume are often scarcely 'poetry' by any (no sonnets, no sestinas, no , no), there are poetical *homages*, notably to Larkin, Yeats and .

in, for example, *Research suggests*, often presents as architecture-on-the-page.

remind of some of Peter Reading's more venturesome . But the (almost) unrelenting rhymelessness and 'de-formity', the the and perhaps above all the continual eschewing of metaphor and seeming lack of sub- or over-text, make any concept of 'total meaning' virtually .

In

in *Zimmer*, for example, Swingler deftly subverts the 'play', the 'Act', the and draws us successfully into , the anti-denouement of which while in *The State*, which – if not explicitly autobiographical, is in some sense in 'confessional' mode – .

Allusions to doodlebugs, too, in more than one poem, appear to be contradicted by

though

Swingler would no doubt argue for the 'supreme fiction' of

since Swingler has

himself stated definitively elsewhere (in

so that to fall into the 'intentional fallacy' would be

.

At his best Swingler offers

and is certainly a near-master of the ellipse and near-blank page. Of fragmentation he has made almost a

.

No other living British poet,

. Swingler's evolution

qua poet, however

. His evolution as a

.

His promised third volume, on 'his' leukaemia, will surely

.

An accidental life

I intended to be born in the second half of the seventh century, of one Finnish parent (of half-Polish, half-Egyptian origin) and one Chinese. My intended mother was poet, weaver, philosopher, prostitute; my father, tinker, wrestler, gamesman, debauch.

I intended to be brought up in ditches and in caravans, singing drunken carousels and gorging sausages of hogs' and bisons' meat, dancing on my head and heels at all the festivals of fire, seducing passing merchants' raven-headed, ivory-skinned daughters, speaking seventeen languages to trade in stones, and be a stirrupless horseman and a master soldier…I intended to be killed aged less than thirty, a mercenary in some African tribal war.

Things did not go according.

I was born, say the records (and they cannot seriously be doubted) in Amersham, Buckinghamshire, England, in the first half of the twentieth century, of seemingly English parents, one 'housewife', one teacher. And there is as yet no death certificate for me, at more than twice my intended age.

A piece of luck

It just so happened
the War was on
still

and he had leave
from the regiment

and she was mid-way
between her periods.

The blackout meant
they didn't feel like
groping their way
to the local fleapit
and, as it happened,

they were still in love,
that Friday at least,

so they made love,
that Friday at least.

I just so happened.

Just my luck.

A piece of calculation

A Labour MP
for a Midlands seat
(later a Minister
for Pensions)
is what he'd always
yearned to be

it just so happened

and it happened also
that she endorsed those
yearnings.

At the *Hog and Hound* that balmy June night, they agreed even his Captain's rank, her Viking beauty and Geordie working class credentials, and their one son (Robin) might not prove enough to spin his election in the Stafford constituency, come war's end.

She told him she was
mid-way between her periods
and though he had his
condoms in his civvies

they agreed this time
to make love without.

In the '45 election, they
used me in the posher,
bluer parts of town:

a cherub on the
doorstep, more convincing
than a flier or
an argument.

First word

It so happened
the War was on
still

and doodlebugs were
dropping into
London

and I was starting to
paddle round your
womb

and that tea-time
you were stretched out
on the divan
in your Holborn studio
flat

and you were reading
Dostoevsky's *Crime and
Punishment*
(can't recall now
quite which page it
was).

It so happened
a blast shook
Mecklenburgh Square
just as

your retinas registered
this single word.

I heard the boom
and saw the word.

Superfluous.

Saviour

It is still War;
I am no more than
early embryo
in my would-be mother's
womb.

She hardly sleeps. She spins round her lathe, at who knows how many revolutions per minute, spraying widgets into pails for guns. When she's not spinning and spraying, she's gabbling to Amy and Caroline that her husband – my would-be father – keeps a mistress up in Cumberland, almost next door to the regimental barracks. She's really overdoing the gin now. She's lying for much too long in scalding-hot baths. How many times have I nearly whooshed it down the tube? Yesterday I was sure I was a gonna when she ran downstairs. I've got to get a message to her.

Even with my embryo brain, I know Morse code, and I know she knows it too. I wait till she's prostrate on the sofa with her latest Russian novel, then

with my embryonic fingers
and my embryonic toes
I tap out the longs and
shorts of my message
on her womb wall:

I WANT OUT
WHOLE AND
AT DUE TIME.

A few minutes later,
she taps something back,
stops,
then repeats.

I get to be born after all.

Perhaps she lives longer, too.

Immaculate birth

It was still
War

and what with Hitler
dropping doodlebugs
on Holborn

(though my would-be mother
had by now done with *Crime
and Punishment*)

there was the question:
Where was I
to be born?

They requisitioned Shardeloes, a Robert Adam mansion near Amersham, at the end of the Metropolitan line, and dismissed the incumbent squire. My mother bore me bloodlessly almost, on a Chippendale couch, beneath a chandelier. For six weeks I scarcely screamed, guzzled happily at breast, neatly soiled my nappy.

*Returned to Holborn,
bustled along in my pram
between raids,*

I turned my face towards
my pillow,
dribbled streams of
milky sick.

Peace and war

Peace – what a thought –
they won't declare.
The war's still fought,
foes everywhere.

Pwhelli
(from a photograph)

This is me on a
beach, digging with
my spade;

nobody else is
there, not even beyond the
breakwater.

There is no
castle or moat, just
hills and hills of
sand.

The sea is
very far out.
It is vanishing
into sky.

My button-up shirt and
long trousers are
flapping in the
wind.

My eyes are fixed on
the spade handle.
I am scowling:

somebody else *is*
there.

'I can do this
sand thing
on my own.'

Rations

'A short back and sides, and a parting on the extreme left, please,' I told Mr Featherstone, the barber/confectioner, and any assembled customers every four weeks bravely, blushing puce though as he always enquired if these were 'Mum's orders'. And then I added: 'Oh, and *loads* and *loads* of Brylcreem.'

When he'd cut it and brushed me and my scarlet blazer down, I pulled out my family ration-book. With my pocket-money pennies, I bought all the sherbert fountains and aniseed balls that were then allowed.

I walked the longest, wrongest, most roundabout way home I could and still be in at five.

If Mum was in (worst luck!) she'd '*Darling, darling*' me, grab me by the wrist, and drag me squealing to the bathroom. Then she'd soap off all my grease.

Unsucked aniseed balls and undrunk sherbert fountains she found on me were snatched away and hidden.

I stabbed her thrust after thrust with my penknife in my head.

When I was nine…

…I made marmalade.

I tore the peel from
scores of bitter little
oranges
and poured the mounds
of sugar
from the scales
into a cauldron
two-thirds the height
of me.
I wore a scarlet
apron that reached my
ankles,

still managing to
dirty shirt and trousers
with the Seville slime.

My mother was
in the kitchen too,
ironing or something.

Mostly I didn't notice
she was there.

The State

If Eton was where
I chose to go,

the local comp,
a 'State',
a block's remove
from Holloway jail,
was where
they sent me,
age eleven,

in the name,
they hectored,
of 'E-
quality'.

From first prayers
at the 'State'
my shins were booted,
my nose fisted,
much more than my mates'

so I bunked off
much more than my mates
and sat out whole Mondays
(and Wednesdays)
in Kings Cross caffs
and neo-Gothic libraries.

I pored over
Caesar's *Gallic Wars,*
Ovid erotica,
Gospel and geometry,
mindless of
the barricaded desks,
the ink-bombs hurled
in Lash's double-Latin,

the flashings
of purple penis-heads
in Harris's Physics,
as he chalked
or wiped the board.

But Eton is where
I chose to go to then

and Eton where
they failed to send me.

Blank I

The writer sits in front of one sheet of blank paper. There is still no sign of the poem about his mother.

Nothing seems impossible to the writer now. The poem about his mother could be sestina or sonnet, the verse free or fixed, the couplets heroic or foot-slogging. A new poetic genre might be born.

The writer decides to write nothing, decides not to consume the paper, decides not to add to the historical sum of other writers' writings.

He just sits in front of his one blank sheet and thinks his thoughts and feels his feelings about his mother. Muses.

No re-writing, editing or proofs required.

Towards the concrete object

'The only way of expressing emotion in the form of art is by finding an "objective correlative";...a set of objects...which shall be the formula of that emotion.'

T S Eliot
The Sacred Wood: Essays on Poetry and Criticism

It's all very well for Eliot, poets of that pedigree.

For me, now, trying to write this about her, it's hard even to name one usable objective correlative.

You see, I don't have access to anything much of hers: just a few cracked Crown Derby cups-and-saucers she gave me eons ago. But then, she's not dead yet.

The first issue, though, surely is: 'What's the feeling I'm hoping to hang onto whatever-it-is?' Then again, can one find *one* objective correlative to hang very mixed feelings on?

I know it's mine, not hers, but perhaps that well-stuffed pillow I dream my head on every night will do after all. There's something protean about a pillow.

Anyway, it'll be a start.

Research suggests

Mothers who

, who

and

are at least twice as

as who do not, according to

, published in , the leading

.

Researchers at the Institute for

studied some 27,000

over a period of

using as controls some , completing the work

in 2009.

unlike their rat counterparts,

human mothers

a Caesarean section.

The

rate of ovarian cancer, though, while

Maternal morbidity rates, taking into account

and the incidence of hysterectomies.

Alcohol played little

even when

.

Breast-feeders were six times more

, especially amongst the

over-forties. Adjusted for

. It made no

difference whether

. Rats, on

the other hand, suffered

.

Mothers generally, according to the figures,

; fathers contributed

.

Earlier findings, which had tended to indicate outcomes
but Dutch and
Canadian research
.

so that national maternity strategies, which

'a social policy
issue for at the very least the next '.

Likeness

At the mirror
sits my mother
Mrs Thatcher
or her brother.

Likeness

At the mirror
sits my mother
Mrs Thatcher
or her brother.

Listen with mother

In full throttle
pre- your strokes
you speechified
on all the politics
of the *Guardian* day.

That strike – right
That war – wrong
you thumped
and that Cabinet swine
should be chopped;
you framed
six reasons why.

I was your dummy
audience then,

developing now-
fashionable skills
of short attention
span.

The politics of acne

My mother just chortled
when I showed her
some of the acne scarring
my adolescent skin.

It had to be
'Eminent Victorians' attitudes
to acne', or
'Acne across Africa'
to induce more than
a cursory word.

I took to doctoring myself
with scores of mail-order
creams and potions,
while our GP
only ever prescribed

more sun.

The depth of skin

Above the Adam's apple
my mother's skin is pink,
cream,
moist
and seamless still,
like her granddaughter
Natasha's.
My mother's never needed
Botox/
topical treatments
squeezed from
fancy tubes.

Her beauty secret,
unbeknownst to her,
is one I am able to pass on:

Let others' fungus
never enter in.

What would you call it then, my love?

But I do love you.
I do.
Of course I do.
You're my mother.
I'm your son.
Don't sons love their mothers?
Aren't they supposed to?

Well, as a son I love you.
Or, I love you as my mother.
Or: 'As a son I love you as a mother.'
You think that sounds too qualified.
Can't you see, though?
There are different kinds of love.
Haven't you heard of 'honouring'?
Of course honouring means something.

OK, I don't phone much.
I know I don't come round much.
No, I don't buy you roses.
So you think I could 'show it more'?
You'd like less talk, more –
But I do love you
or honour you at least.

Alright, you do irritate me sometimes.
Alright, you irritate me continually.
And you frustrate me.
You subvert me.
Yes, you can be quite noxious.
As you say, you're by no means the perfect mother.
We can agree on that.
But I do love you.
Irrespective, yes, irrespective.

No, not all the time.
Not continuously.
Not when you're noxious for instance.
Yes, that's fair: I love you 'on the whole'.
OK: 'I love you generally speaking.'

You think I think too much.
You think my love is more thought than feeling.
You think it's all 'in my head'.
What's wrong with that, though, if I do love you as a son?

You don't look convinced.
You don't believe I love you at all, do you?
I *am* telling you the truth.

Look, as far as I know, I love you.

So it's a peculiar kind of love.
What would you call it then, my love?

No competition

Incest: that never was
our problem, at least
on my side.

You were always
very tall and
very blonde and
very busty and
very shrill

and ever since you
pinned my nappies, well,
you failed to stir me
there.

Dad could keep you,
and he did. Unless I err,
there was nothing

Freudian about us.

One kind of family

My family?
You mean
the one I come *from*?

Well, I do have a
mother, and I did have a
father, and yes
they/we did live together –
until he
died, that is.

There were four of us –
siblings, that is.
As you say, a
nuclear family.

Hey, did you say
nuclear?

The school of home

Did they house you; did they keep you warm?
Yes, I always had a room, a roof, and I was warm enough. In those ways, there never was neglect.

Did they allow you to climb trees when you said you wanted to?
Yes, they did, though the almost branchless ones were taxing. When I fell, they would not wash or dress my wounds.

Did they, when you were of an age, instruct you in the facts, so-called, of life?
Yes, in their way they did. They left on my bed, though without a note to say they had, a very fingered copy of a book. *The Wonder of Life* had little text, was mostly diagram and illustration.

Did your father teach you how to shave?
Yes, through the bathroom door he rarely closed, I watched him lather up his foam, brush on and often cut himself.

How were family Sundays spent?
At dinner, my mother craved some praise for her apple charlotte; my father carved without a word. Away from table, he read me my misdemeanours of the week, according to her reckoning. That heard, I slunk to my room, turned the key in the door, and hugged my bakelite radio.

How did they guide you on what you would do beyond your leaving home?
I'd fastened on The Law somehow as the profession I would follow. They paid the fees for me to learn that law, and when they remembered asked me what marks I'd got for papers sat.

Was there love between them, *do you think?*
I think so, yes. Whenever I took their breakfast to their room, they always were propped up snug together in their bed.

Were you (are you) 'well-brought-up'?
Was I much 'brought-up' at all? I largely raised myself. Or dropped me down.

In memoriam *my father, MP*

He had sleek black hair and stood like a Guard in his forty-shilling Burton suit.

The lungs of his constituency miners were his foremost surgery concern;

later, as the Minister, he moved a Transport Bill vote by vote through the Commons part.

Sundays he carved the beef at the family table, if the *Express* didn't ring for a Moscow point of view.

His secret was a revolver, German, a trophy of the War, kept below the finest linen in a chest,

his own best weapon his handwriting: tiny, cursive, and unteachably beautiful.

In memoriam *my father*

He never taught me car-engines, chess, Maths, or how to shave;

would not cast a judgement on the Beatles, Stones or Who.

He boxed me on the head for sins that were not specified,

and in a cricket friendly span me out first ball without apology.

He scarcely ever called me by my name and, when he died,

of too much Parliament, I missed what I had missed for all my
life.

A new strip

If only the family were more like a football team. Unhappy at left back? Unhappy with your present contract? Give your parent-bosses notice. Re-sign as a striker, for a club in a Brazilian league,

but one with a lighter
strip.

Robin

The oldest of us, in this respect, did the rightest thing.

Five wartime years, from ages one to six, strangers far from home fostered him and called him son. With peace, his natural parents shipped him back. A brother, me, had not long been born; soon, other siblings came.

Twelve years more he lived with us, enough to come to judgement on the failings of our family blood and genes. Acute psychologist already, he then trained to be one.

The other three of us serially made and broke, made and broke, relationships, fathering and mothering as we made and broke. Robin practised what Larkin in his infamous poem preached: 'And don't have any kids yourself.'

Avoiding having 'kids himself', Robin married a woman with a family ready-made, and fostered them – we say *as if* – he'd been their real or natural dad. He schooled four children from the nursery to their respective times of leaving home. They flourished as he nurtured as they grew.

In our family, the oldest sibling did the rightest thing.

He proved the best of parents.

Oliver

We're brothers, family. I'm the second-born. You came fourth and last. We're brothers: we've that common source of blood and gene.

You were very silent when we were two sons at home, and chess was what we always played.

I won those games invariably. And I smirked as, pre-empting my mate, you toppled your own King.

Then, in our thirties, you set me right about those silent adolescent wars. You always could – you claimed – have beaten me, but chose restraint and resignation. And what you said was no doubt true: you had such ease with calculus and calculations.

Since teenage times it's been less meet than gap between us,

and now that you're a hermit, almost, in your distant social-housing scheme, we may not shake the other's hand again,

not even at her funeral.

Hiatus

Since my sister
and I
have not been
speaking,
I have relished the

hiatus,

that little extra

space.

Now I'm trusting my
address book
to reveal

Christmas-card-relatives
and friends-who-aren't

so I'll have still fewer

lines

to write

or say.

Material girl

More milk for her,
less for her siblings,
that's been my sister's creed.

She is big,
and they are small:
Each according to her need.

Sighting

We were some thirty yards apart, but it must have been her: that slouching in the trunk, the bloodless cheeks, sunglasses on a sunless day. My eyes narrowed, trying to make the image out, let the brain be sure. My feet were not so patient. *Staccato* turn-round, they marched my whole body back towards the Tube.

My feet well know now that my ears believe no words heard from the mouth of my sister.

Our animal farm

Our family said
as mealtime grace:
'Two breasts – good,
two balls – bad.'

Breast fed boy

If I am a man now,
was it the mother's
milk
that helped to make me so?

If I am a man now,
what was it
in
the mother's milk
that helped to make me so?

If I am a boy still,
had it
turned –
the mother's milk –
to help keep me
so?

As good as

As good as dead till later middle age,
at last I dared to breathe a heartfelt word,
wrenched my body from the prisoner's cage
to sing. But all had flown and no one heard.

On the Kilburn High Road

Amongst the
pavement babble of
numberless
alien

tongues,
I **STOMP** and
RANT alone,
CURSING my

kin and kith
forever
to stink-holes
in the ground

and pass
unheeded there,
more bluntly –
quite ignored.

Blank II

The writer sits in front of one sheet of blank paper. There is still no sign of another poem about his mother.

Nothing seems impossible to the writer now. This poem about his mother could be sestina or sonnet, the verse free or fixed, the couplets heroic or foot-slogging. A new poetic genre might be born.

The writer decides to write nothing again, decides not to consume the paper, decides not to add to the historical sum of other writers' writings.

He just sits in front of his one blank sheet again and thinks his thoughts and feels his feelings about his mother. Muses.

As before, no re-writing, editing or proofs required.

Last Christmas

Though not once in her life has she been *incontrovertibly* ill to our combined knowledge, on *anno domini* grounds alone surely we, her four adult children, have unspokenly seemed to agree every Christmas since '89: 'This Christmas must be her last.'

And so every Christmas since '89 we've all scrawled extra kisses on the bottoms of our cards to her, and on the Day itself we've creamed the brandy butter for her and decanted the bread sauce for her, and all Day we've swallowed our own spleen.

It's Boxing Day 2007. We're still swallowing. She's still feeding and breathing.

Mother alone

On the distant screen,
Jon Snow, *compère*
of the evening's news.

A Zimmer frame,
stranded
on a desert of
pea–
green carpet.

A yesterday's
Guardian,

on a stool,
open at the quick
crossword.

On a tray,
with a single
cube of ice,
a Gordon's
gin.

A high-bottomed
armchair.

The TV remote,
under the coffee-
table.

And a mobile

nowhere in the
room.

Portrait of my mother as a very old woman

The hair is wholly silver, wholly matt. Each so-thin strand has been lacquered into its space and would remain there in your windless, torpid room, except that with the left hand you preen the scalp continually.

The cheeks are the high if unperspiring red which they have been always with you, but the more so now from the swilling of gin or from roasting the skin hours at a time by the mock coal fire.

The bone in your nose keeps it Roman straight, and the nostrils dilate in time with your rhetoric and ranting.

Even your most maniacal or hysterical laugh does not prise open the mouth enough to reveal its missing molars, though it does expose teeth with brown stainings from long-time tea-drinking and, doubtless, other origins.

The non-white parts of the eyes show a cold white too, as if you were blind almost, and the eyeballs rove in their sockets, without seeming to look.

Your clothes are loose and transparent. Under your blouse, the bosom (the breasts no longer separate) folds down towards the belly. The waist has descended to the hip. The thighs have shrunk to be commensurate with the calves. The toes curl inwards as you stand, so the feet do not hold up the trunk so well as the stalk of neck holds up the head.

Smoking, you scarcely grasp your cigarette between the fingers. The veins of the hand bulge a ghastly green and black.

Through the bedroom window

Through her bedroom window,
till they're beyond sight,
she tracks the passing buggies from
her wheelchair, pausing only

to stare back at the mantleshelf
montage of photos framed:
four children, no longer children,
posing some on beaches, some in blazers.

The agency carer steers a trolley,
china cups, teapot on its dedicated mat.
From the latest buggie shifting into focus,
a single piercing yelp. 'My third

yelped like that, my dear, when
I didn't feed her cheese. They
were called prams then. She
grew up so rosy, so pretty, though.'

The whitening

At the age of ninety-two
our mother will
next Wednesday
limp into the surgery
for her dental whitening.

There's no lover
that we know of
but our mother does like
to smile

and, as she says,
she's flush now
(money from that equity-
release)

and the wisdoms
are included.

Permanent wave

Your sole outing now
is to the hairdresser's;
your live-in daughter drives you.

At 3 pm they paint bleach compound on
your skull, park you in the corner under
the battery of wheeled heaters. At 4 pm
or so your scalp emerges as a froth of curls.
And if the wave they give you is not
permanent,

the life you have does seem to be
so.

One reason to live

(after words by W B Yeats)

My mother now
is very very old
and very very grey
and should be
very very full of sleep.

But her eyes
are still wide
for Jon Snow
and his TV
news at seven.

And every evening
my mother refuses
to die.

Marbles

My mother and her marbles:
I fear she's losing them.
In the air they're tossed

and stay there.

Good enough son

If I be more the parent now
since you be more the child
you surely will be trusting now
that I will prove more mild.

Power of attorney

Mum,

no, I haven't come to shoot you

I've brought that

'Notice' document,

you know, the
one I mentioned
before,

really, I haven't come to shoot you

to do with

you not having to
do things like

sign cheques
anymore.

Honestly,

you don't need to
look at it now.
After the news,
yes.

Mum, I'm not
staying this time.

Mum, you know I
let myself in.

No, I haven't come to shoot you.

This poem
(after a poetic idea by Andrew Motion)

This poem about my mother
has nothing to do with politics,
the *Guardian's* or any other

leaders. It is a poem about
my mother. About an old lady
and her arthritic toes, without

too many callers. She longs to die;
the smokes should help. Ponder
it enough and you could cry.

The hardest words

'Forgive'?
That's the first time you've used *that* word.
Ah, you used it because you thought that was what *I* meant.
So, not because *you* think you've done anything 'wrong'.
You don't *necessarily* think you have.
Though you *may* have done.
You think *I* think you at least *may* have done.

But you're waiting for *me* to say what it is you've done.
And you're worried – alright, that's not quite the word –
about the term 'wrong'.
Of course, wrong's not quite the same as sin.
Of course, wrong's not necessarily crime.
Yes, I do know you're not 'religious'.
Look, wrong's the best I can come up with.

Except that, I'm not talking about just one wrong.
Yes, it's more in the nature of a list.
Yes, and rather a long list.
No, I haven't got 'the list' on me, I haven't even made up the
list yet.
OK, I'll draw up my list; no, not now, my notes are somewhere
else.
I'll draw up the list, then you study it at your leisure and tick
where you agree 'you've done something wrong'.

You've got a better formula.
You'll tick where you agree that you *harmed* me, even though
you don't necessarily feel to *blame*.
You're prepared to say sorry even though you won't
necessarily feel to blame.
OK, that's strange, but OK.

Where are we up to?
When you've ticked where you agree you harmed me, you say
sorry on each count, then I can 'forgive' on each count.
As you say – I agree – whatever 'forgive' really means.

We'll both say the words.
We may not *feel* the words much, but we can *say* the words.
The more we say the words, the more we say the words, as you
say, eventually, eventually –
Feelings are 'for later', yes, that's well-said.

Then we can start again, slate clean.
Or – as you say – not.
We might agree never to see one another again.
Or – as you say – not.

But the slate'll be clean.
The slate *will* be clean.

Fragmentary remains of a letter (thought to be from son to mother) decomposed through damp

Dea

'Forgive'? That's not the

You've committed no cr

cot, rape

single ac

bore me, fed me, cloth

schooled

son, not God

incompat

you are old now and

dredged an

standoff' draw a line und o
change

ragged rui
ti
time wil

sorry sorr
ever agai

Zimmer

(A play in one Act)

Scene one. A sitting room

The Zimmer stands on the carpet.

The carpet is not made of wool.
It is not made of cotton.
It was not made abroad.
It is not unfrayed.

The Zimmer is not made of brass.
It is not made of lead.
It is not last year's model.
It weighs no more than a litre of milk.

The clock on the coffee-table shows 4.01 pm

The Zimmer continues to face the mantlepiece.
It remains some two feet from the television screen.
It remains some twelve feet from the sitting-room door.

It is untouched by any hand.

And the carpet continues to support the Zimmer, the coffee-table, the television and all the objects of the room.

Scene two. A master bedroom

A woman is lying in bed.

The bed is not a Slumberland or Dreamland bed.
The woman was not born in 1922 or 1923.
Her name is not Clare.
It is not Natasha.
The woman's eyes are not closed.
She does not touch the Zimmer.

The clock on the coffee-table shows 4.21 pm

The woman is not reading her Susan Hill novel or wearing her velvet housecoat.
Her eyes are fixed on the complex ceiling plasterwork.
She is not now thinking of any one of her three living sons.
She is not yet 110.
The woman does not feel unwell in any definable way.
She is not aware of suffering from any kind of malignant neoplasm of the stomach or nephrotic syndrome.

The house doorbell is not rung.

The clock on the coffee-table now shows 4.44 pm

Scene three. A second bedroom

A second woman, an agency carer, is sitting in the armchair,
not listening to Sixties hits through her headphones.
The agency is not called Urban Uncles.
It is not called English Aunts.
The carer is from neither New Zealand nor South Africa.

The clock on the coffee-table now shows 4.54 pm

The Zimmer frame remains on the carpet in the sitting room.

Scene four. The master bedroom. Nine minutes later

The woman lying in her bed pushes herself up very slowly and makes as if to stand. She suddenly loses strength in her left arm, falls towards a sharp edge in her bedside chest-of-drawers, and cracks open her head.

How is your mother?

Very well, thank you;
she's very well.
Fine,
yes.

No, she's alright –
really.
Well, not so bad.
So-so, you know.

Actually –
Actually –
since you ask –
she's not so well.
Quite *un*well, in fact.
If you want the truth.

She had a fall.
No, she didn't break anything, but –

Yes, the doctor's been.
Yes, her doctor's good.
Yes, he came almost at once.

An 'attack', he said –
no, I can't remember the word –
some kind of 'attack'.

She's in bed –
no, still at home.
She can't articulate clearly.
Yes, very very confused.
Not in a state to have visitors.

They don't know.
They don't seem to know.
They're saying they don't know.
It's too early to say.
Anything at her age, of course –
No, she's ninety-two now; yes.

Lucky?
Not to have broken anything?
Yes, I suppose you're right.
But she doesn't look good.
'Like death' is how I'd put it;
yes, *that* pale.
Yes, I am worried, you're right.

Apart from that –
Apart from that,
if there is an 'apart from that' –

Anyway, you did ask.
Thanks for asking.

And you?
How are you, then?
Oh, and how is Mary?

A short life forwards

War-time.

Born Matthews, *Tyneside*, poor.
Left.

Peace.
London.
Worked and paid,
worked and paid,
worked and paid
(taxes).

Good-looker:
met man:
Labour man:
loved man:
married man.
Born Matthews,
turned Swingler.

Labour girl.

Peace still – just.
Fucked and bore.

War again.
Fucked and bore.

Peace again again.
Fucked and bore,
fucked and bore,
presto!
a family of four.

Cooked and chored,
cooked and chored,
cooked and chored,
cooked and chored.

Swingler-man died.
Swingler-man died:
poor again:
worked and paid,
worked and chored,
cooked and paid
(taxes).

London still,
London always;
never left,
never left.
Peace still,
still *peace.*
Got old,
went white:
what a chore,
oh, what a bore!

Began to fail,
began to falter
began to

fall

fall

fall

fall.

That's all.

Unheroic couplet

'Everything that is,' wrote Pope, 'is right.'
My mother's dead and I shall sleep tonight.

Unheroic quatrain

At long last I'm an orphan;
at long last Mum is dead.
I'm alone, I'm on a pension but
now I get to have my head.

The Guardian

The *Guardian* reminds me.

Early Victorian stucco reminds me.

Glenda Jackson and Mrs Thatcher

and *Carmen* and *Salome*

and Rider Haggard's *She*

and radio debates on Nature v Nurture

and Pwhelli and Sri Lanka

and Zimmer frames

and shocks of all-white hair

remind me.

Six letters of the alphabet in a certain order remind me (as if I could forget).

She is everywhere.

Even I *remind me of my mother.*

The solicitor speaks to the family

The last words
your mother spoke,

I am to say,

and to deny,
pre-emptively,
that they are
apocryphal,

are
as set out
on the one
sheet
in the brown
envelope
you all have
to hand.

Please proceed now
to open your
envelope,
read,
and commit the
twenty-seven words
to memory.

When you have all
signalled completion,

please follow me
to the office
shredder.

Not waiting

'Dear Mr Swingler,'
the solicitor addressed me
on a cream bond paper
with a twelve-digit
reference-code,
adding yesterday's
date.

'   I am sorry for the delay in
                    probate   I am now finally in a position
to
                                        .

'   I trust that you will appreciate that your
mother's
                                        and a surprising parallel fall in
                    and after thirteen bequests to various relations and
          so that the great bulk of her estate
                                        and, as you will see from the enclosed,
inheritance tax at   as well, of course, as our own firm's
                                        .

'This leaves   , of which your
                                        .

'If you will now kindly sign the enclosed slip, which
, we will be able to

.

.

'If you have any

'

He signed himself off
with a Yours sincerely.

I returned my
slip.

Fortunately, I'd been
busy with business.
I had not been
waiting.

No comparison

There's been no Ian
Paisley in our family

to my knowledge

nor a Gerry
Adams

but since those
righteous, speechful
bomb-
asts
finally kissed and
made it up
in Ulster

how I've missed
my simile!
Help!

Now I rake
the foreign pages of
The Times and
Guardian

for a State
as riven now

as our house was.

Dear doctor

Dear doctor,
This is just to confirm to you what I said at the end of our trial session the other day, viz. that I will *not* now be coming to see you for Freudian-style psychoanalysis five times a week at 7am, 50 minutes a session, each session costing £100 (non-negotiable, no concessions), indefinitely as you yourself said, and again as you said, with no guarantee of my greater happiness or any successful outcome.

I had thought that Freudian-style psychoanalysis might be especially suitable for me, rooted as my present problems are in wretched early relationships with mother/father/siblings and now other significant-others. Unfortunately, my 'present problems' include my total incapacity to pay your fees now or at any foreseeable time.

Since the National Health Service does not seem to provide what you thought I needed, clearly I am going to have to lie on my own couch, metaphorically speaking, spend more time looking at myself in the mirror, literally and metaphorically, interpret my own dreams, which as you know I do write up and keep, (though never once, oddly, has there been a dream including my mother in any recognisable guise), and trust to catharsis in any outlets I can find, from fencing to poetry-writing. 'The lion within' you referred to at our session is clearly an animal I am going to have to hunt down and tame quite on my own.

There is no need to reply to this, unless you feel I have misrepresented our meeting to your professional detriment.

Yours sincerely,

Bridesmaid

Suicide had been popular in his extended family, but so far he had always been the 'bridesmaid'.

Mostly without success, admittedly, brother, sister, cousin and others had attempted it. Some had used gas, which was an option then. Others had chivvied at wrists with razors. Others still had pestled miscellanies of pills from bathrooms and parental chests-of-drawers and whisked cocktails, adding their alcohol of choice.

Then, these efforts unrewarded, thwarted by speeding ambulance crews, there he would reliably be, at their bedside, UCH, Royal Northern, Royal Free, holding their hands if bandage and plaster allowed, trying not to ask the wrong questions through the clatter of trolleys.

Later, when their bodies had been partly mended, they mostly travelled north, to a hospital caring more for mind and soul than body. Here also he was to be found, listening and listening and listening away, or seeming to.

Despite the encouragement of all these family members, and the fashion for (at least) the deed attempted, he always failed somehow to transcend what doctors call 'ideation'. In his mind, he would often throw himself from some notorious high bridge, and sometimes he did keep a pair of open scissors by his bed, but he signally failed to act.

He lacked the gene for it.

Many happy returns, Mum!
London. AD 2314.

- London is now an independent Muslim state. What was England has now been divided into four provinces.

- There are 797 mosques. The Church of England was disestablished in 2119, and now claims no more than 300 'adherents'. There is a new religion called Paradeism.

- The population is now doubling every twenty-six years, and habitations increasingly are built underground.

- The city is now the eighty-ninth richest state in the world, immediately behind Bulmania and Gobistan.

- The average August daytime temperature is now 49°C.

- Westminster Abbey was demolished in 2206 to make way for a textiles market. Tower Bridge was demolished last year.

- Pigeons are extinct. Hawks, vultures and varieties of parrot are now the commonest species.

- Plane trees have died out. There are three hornbeams in one street in London NW. Coconut trees line what was once Pall Mall.

It is your 400th birthday. You have listed-person status, and in the flat where you have lived for almost all your life you raise a glass of Bolivarian rummygin with the assembled guests, none of whom is ethnically 'old English'.

'Immortality is an option,' you proclaim, puffing at a Marlboro Reserve. 'Yes, a good constitution helps, but otherwise it is the way one lives one's life. Yes, seventy-six years ago I had a scare, something to do with my kidneys, they said, but I'm over that now.'

A consultant immortality-gerontologist nods vigorously, fanning you with a bonsai banana-plant.

The complaint of the would-be cathartic writer

His book is out. The bad blood's let. The shit's been shat.

Uncounted green-headed boils have been lanced. Endless strings of phlegm have been spat out, endless streams of bile vomited up, almost the spleen itself. Surely now he has drained from his body for good all that was fit to drain...

but it is not so, of course. Bad blood pumps back in again. Shit solidifies once more in inner passages. The old green boils were lanced from the face; new scarlet ones re-form on the buttocks and the backs of thighs. A fresh bile tastes bitterer even than it did before...

so, once embarked on his endeavour, the writer is condemned, just to keep free of re-occurring toxins, to a whole *life* of fabricating books,

only his death-breath his true catharsis.

Index

Swingler, Stephen Thomas.

not intended father of Nicholas   9
not 'tinker, wrestler, gamesman or debauch'   9
not Finnish or Chinese   9

absence from marmalade making sessions in the Swingler household   23

actual father of Nicholas, according to records   9

absence from Nicholas's complaints about his adolescent acne   35

no competition from Nicholas for the sexual favours of Anne Swingler   39

spending less time with his family   44

as a man who did not teach his son car-engines   45
as a teacher, according to records   9
as a Captain (*Army*)   11
as a spin bowler (*cricket*)   45
as a carver of beef   44
as a believer in 'Equality'   24
as a Minister (*Government*)   44

See also

Absence
Love
Sex
Clare (*daughter*)
Robin (*son*)
Oliver (*son*)
Nicholas (*son*)
Eton
Schools, State
Regiment (*Army*)
The War
Express
Cherubs
1945